Minimalist Lifestyle:

A Beginners Guide to Simple Living. Learn Everything From Budgeting To Decluttering and Much More

Table of Contents

Introduction

I want to thank you and congratulate you for downloading the book A Beginners Guide to Simple Living. Learn Everything from Budgeting To Decluttering and Much More

This book contains proven steps and strategies on how to live a fulfilling but simple life. Stop being a slave to your possessions! Stop being the cash cow of capitalist oligarchs. Stop working day in and day out only to have a couple of hour's happiness in buying new things you don't really need. Haven't you noticed it yet? You want this and want that. You then slave away more than 8 hours each day, working at a job you don't enjoy doing, in order to buy that product. Once the novelty of the purchase wears off, it gets relegated to a spot in your closet, attic, or garage. You watch television and you see something else you want and the cycle continuous. The same goes for services like premium cable, faster internet connectivity, higher phone plans, etc. You don't really need all that. But you think that not buying into it deprives you of enjoying the pleasure of your hard earned cash.

Here's an inescapable fact: By wanting more, you work longer hours, thus depriving yourself the time to enjoy life and the company of your family. Here is a simple example: Do you remember the time when you had a single television set in your home and there were no laptops, tablets and cellular phones? The author vividly remembers this. The author spent most of the days outdoors, playing with friends, exploring the neighborhood, swimming at lakes, etc. At home, watching TV was a family thing. You only have one set situated in the living room, so all of you had to gather there, interact with each other, and talking to each other.

In this highly industrialized and commercialized age, ask any adult what the source of his a/her trouble is, and one of the top three answers will be related to shortage of income vis a vis inability to buy what he/she was brainwashed into thinking as "the luxuries of life".

If you do not develop your individualistic thought, sense of outdoor adventure, and financial savvy, you will continue to be a slave to commercials, print ads, the fad of the day, etc. The most apparent result is a very cluttered home. Less apparent is a cluttered mind, and a weighted down soul.

It's time for you to become an amazing person who is in control of his/her finances. This eBook will show you how. The author believes in a realistic approach to minimalism. As such, we don't expect you to go cold, uncluttered turkey overnight. Realistically speaking, you can adapt one aspect of this eBook at a time; say one each week. After a year you'll find yourself less stressed, happier, and living in a much more comfortable home. Of course, if you want to speed up the process a bit, realistically, 3 months is enough time to see substantial results.

Read with an open mind, enjoy!

Chapter 1: What is a Minimalist Lifestyle?

If you ask a lay man, what a minimalist lifestyle is, he/she will probably answer in terms of home design and sparse but stylish furnishings. Granted, this is correct, but is only a single aspect, and arguably, the most superficial aspect of minimalism. You want to go deeper!

Minimalism is About Freedom NOT Restrictions

This is arguably the most important aspect of minimalism. The average Joe/Jane will probably define minimalism as a means of restricting your possessions, income, luxury, etc. In reality, minimalism is a shift in lifestyle wherein you stop prioritizing unnecessaries and putting more effort into yourself and your natural surroundings. In other words, you remove the clutter in order to make room for something better in your life. Therefore, simply throwing away stuff and having, sparse, albeit stylish furniture will not cut it.

The American Dream is Too Burdensome

If you ask the average Joe "What the American dream is?" You'll probably get an answer similar to this "Make more money so I don't have to want for anything". The first part is the essence of it all "to make more money". The fallacy is the second part, which is "not to want anything". This is because, the way a capitalist society is structured, everyday something "new" is offered for sale. What is worst, you are conditioned to believe that you want, sometimes even need, a product or service.

For example: Jane Doe has just bought a popular Orange myphone 5. After 6 months, Orange releases a "new" phone, the Orange myphone 5s. The sad part is, the features on the 5s is almost the same. It is only that, there is more memory on the myphone 5s. This is something that did not require new technology and could have been added to the myphone 5. Thru clever advertising, Jane Doe now wants the new phone. And because she is living the American lifestyle she should not want for anything. She buys it, despite the fact that it will probably be paid via credit card on installment. Now Jane has 2 phones. She then keeps the older phone in her drawer gathering dust, together with her myphone3, myphone 3s, myphone 4, myphone 4s. Incidentally, all are perfectly working smart phones. Whatever happened to using something until it breaks, or is cheaper to replace! The bottom-line is, nowadays, manufacturers often shortchange buyers by selling products that are not their best. This way the buyer has to pay another sum to upgrade.

Minimalism is Different for Each Person

The most basic definition of a true minimalist is "someone who lives a fulfilling life, knowing what he/she needs, having the resources to amass those requirements, and achieving happiness within. The definition is barely instructional, yet vaguely profound.

It all hinges on a person letting go of preconceptions and societal norms, and knowing what makes him/her happy. This means, one minimalist my need a car to go to and from work while the other only needs a bicycle or a healthy pair of legs. A minimalist may live in the mountains with only his/her books while another may live within the city with a full array of job related electronics.

It's a Step by Step Process

Throwing away all your earthly possessions is not minimalism. That's just foolhardy. Minimalism can start with one person de-cluttering a refrigerator. After a week, that same person starts advertising on Craigslist, for the disposal for sale or for free of unnecessary home furnishings. After a month, the same person starts collecting clothes he/she has not worn for a year, and giving it to charity. The next month, unnecessary utilities and premium cable, internet connectivity and postpaid phone lines are disconnected. The trick is to part with the things you do not need without feeling deprived of the same and knowing deep down inside that other people have a better use for your pre loved items. Eventually you will start de cluttering your mind from the useless wish list you have on amazon.com or similar sites. That extra burden eases your mind. This minimizes the need for cash, which in turn allows you to think clearly on what you want to do with your life, are you happy with your current job, or are you in it for the hefty salary?

Necessary Spending

The author has a different approach to minimalism than some. In that, letting go of earthly possessions and unnecessary worries does not mean being foolhardy and leaving things to luck. For example, keeping your HMO and savings account for emergencies and retirement is part of being a minimalist. Paying for an ivy league college tuition fee is also an investment for the future that need not be skimped on. The occasional box of pizza, family night out, and movie night is also a part of being a minimalist. Yes, you should learn to enjoy nature but you should also learn not to deprive yourself of simple pleasures and harmless rewards.

For example: There is nothing wrong with paying a premium to buy a tablet PC that allows you to connect reliably to family member's abroad. There is something wrong with wanting a tablet PC when you have a laptop in good working order and can do the job just as well.

Familial Connections

Minimalism is supposed to allow you to reconnect to family and friends. This is by removing distractions and allowing you to built deeper bonds. This presupposes you furnish a part of your home or find a suitable place for your family to get together. Move your family back to the living and dining room and out of their individual rooms.

A Cup Half Full

Remember the saying about the optimist and pessimist. The former says "the glass is half empty" while the latter says "the glass is half full". The superficial minimalist says "there is ½ more glass than is needed". A real minimalist says "there is just enough water, to allow something else inside".

In other words, it is not about trimming your capacity for income to live with the bare minimum. That's just being a pauper! Minimalism is about removing what you do not need in order to allow other more important things to enter your life!

Straight Line Towards Happiness

Simply put, minimalism is knowing the real you and your household. After that, it's all about navigating thru life in a straight line towards real happiness and fulfillment. This is done with as little distractions as possible by foregoing unnecessaries.

Chapter 2: Pros and Cons of Minimalism?

Minimalism is something that can work for every person in society. This is not total deprivation, but rather a realization of what is truly important and a commitment to steer one's whole being. Commitment is key, and others cannot fully do so or are lacking in proper knowledge that they think it is too hard to commit.

This chapter will try to remove those doubts by discussing the pros and cons of minimalism. Make your own determination. Just a simple reminder, there is nothing wrong with taking things slow. And stopping halfway is still better than not taking the first step.

-Clutter Free Home vs. Decluttering Your Home

A minimalist lifestyle can allow you to maximize your living space by minimizing surplus items inside your home i.e. furniture, clothes, kitchen appliance and utensils, etc. This makes it more comfortable for you and your household in the long run because you have more space to move. It's also very easy on the eyes because the less you own the less clutter that you see.

The problem is, the Decluttering process can get a bit stressful. You need to sort out your things and let go of the same. Some go to charity, others can be given to relatives and friends. Do you think you can handle that?

-Spend Less vs. Less Material Possessions

Think of a minimalist as a sharpshooter. A minimalist patiently waits and targets specific needs and then executes a purchase. This usually means that items you buy are more expensive but are of higher quality and utility. For example, John Doe purchases a touch screen laptop instead of a tablet pc. This is because the former can do almost anything the latter can and then some.

On the other hand, you have less of everything. This means you share your items with your other household member. The solution is to schedule the use of a laptop, watching television, or using the family car. This is not deprivation but interaction with relationship mechanics.

-Clean Living vs. Minimal Cleaning Tools

Knick knacks gather dust. The more possessions you have, the harder it is to clean your home. The less possessions you have, the easier it is to clean. Based on experience, since you no longer dread the chore of cleaning your home, you do it more often.

Most minimalists have a select few cleaning implements. For example, you have a broom and dust pan instead of a vacuum cleaner. Why no vacuum cleaner? Well, Most are bulky, and unless your home is predominantly carpeted, you don't really need it.

-Be More Productive vs. No Distractions

Have you ever felt like there isn't enough hours in a day for you to finish   everything you want to do? Why don't you list down your schedule for the day. How much of your time is wasted by gadgets, gizmo's, internet, etc.? For example:

- Your favorite game Halo 4 got released. This meant a couple of hours of hours wasted on game play.

- Ever heard of flappy bird? How many minutes of your time did you waste on trying to get that ugly bird thru those pipes.

- Have you ever switched on the television, started watching a show on cable, and just had to finish several episodes in one sitting?

Without those gadgets, gizmo's and other modern day clutter and time wasters, you actually have plenty of time in a single day!

-Earth Friendly vs. Economy 101

Simply put, minimalists consume less. If a majority of individuals were so, then we would be cutting less trees, consuming less petrol, emitting less carbon dioxide. On the other hand, consumption is tied with economic stability. The less a society consumes, the harder it is for the economy to go up.

However, some economists argue that, if consumers consume less, then the producers will be forced to provide better value, in order to be competitive. If these producers were to target minimalists, then this would result in higher quality and more utility.

-Be a Good Example

Show the next generation the proper way to consume/utilize goods and services! Make them understand that every purchase must be well thought out. This in turn will become a trend for future generations to follow.

-Past vs. Future

Majority of the clutter in your home comprise of old clothes, old furniture, kitchen wares and utensil, etc. Yes, that baby crib might hold some sentimental value. Yes, that shirt was a gift from your ex. Yes, those old magazines, take you back to your childhood. But you no longer need the same. Why don't you give it to charity to be used by other children or families who are down on their luck! Don't forget the past. Be grounded on the present and look forward to the future.

-Personalize Your Home vs. What Others May Say

By owning less, you are forced to choose things you truly cherish. These are the things that will eventually fill your home. A simple and sturdy sofa and side table with the pictures of your family looks better than one filled with dusty and newspapers, throw pillows, keys, moldy scented candles. In other words, you showcase yourself in your home, not your clutter.

Some would argue that having less possessions may lead others to the wrong idea that you are strapped for cash. To this, minimalists say, "so what?" Let them think what they want to think. You know better, and if they question your finances, you could always explain to them your fundamental belief in minimalism.

Chapter 3: Slowly But Surely

Congratulations on deciding to de-clutter your life. This chapter will focus on how you can slow integrate a minimalist lifestyle to the status quo. This is a no nonsense approach. The author chooses to start internally before external acts.

Clear Your Mind of the Unnecessary

The problem is, differentiating the necessary from the unnecessary. There is no one set rule in order to do this. All the author can provide is a very useful hack, and several guidelines:

- Keep a journal. Start writing down your daily schedule. After a week of entries you should have a pretty good idea on how you spend your days.

- Separate each activity into important, less important, waste of time, etc. At the onset, try to half the time you spend on time wasters. Don't stop there; continue until you cut the same by 90%. Realistically speaking 10% will remain. Although, in the long run, you will eventually trim that figure some more.

- Wake up with the sun! By waking up early you can do all sorts of important things.

- Relish the start of your day. Have you noticed; you wake up earlier when you have something important to do, or something you want to do. This way you won't be hitting the snooze button on your alarm.

- End the day with a flourish. Think of something special to cap your day off. It doesn't need to be expensive or exotic. The author likes to finish his day with a slice of cake and red wine.

De Clutter Yourself

Try this simple exercise. After a full day's work, what do you have in your immediate person, pockets, bag, car, etc.? In other words, how much clutter do you carry on you on a day to day basis? How much clutter do you collect after a full day's work? More importantly, where to you place/store the same?

For example, usually you have fresh batch of pennies, and loose change. You have a few receipts, candy wrappers, food wrappers, cups, tissue, a magazine, etc. First you need a place to store the clutter i.e. piggybank or throw it away i.e. useless receipts. You do not just store it inside your drawer because after a couple of weeks, your place will be messy again!

Minimalism and Your Day Job

Your job plays an important role in your peace of mind. Ask yourself this simple question "Do I enjoy my work?" "Do I look forward to tomorrow on the weekends?" "Do I see myself working here for 10, maybe 20 years?" Just to be clear, the author is referring to your job per se, not your co-workers. That's another item on your checklist.

If your answer is no, then you should seriously consider changing your department, or employer. Don't do it on a whim. Go job hunting and only resign after you get a feasible job offer. By feasible, it means, even if you earn less for now but there is room for professional and income growth.

Minimalism and Family

A minimalist lifestyle is best lived by your entire household. However, you should not force something, no matter how appealing it is, on anyone else. The best thing you can do is show them the merits of minimalism.

Of course, if you are the principal breadwinner, you have a little bit more leeway to impose your will. But try to be reasonable. Remember, it's harder for kids to live this sort of lifestyle. But if you inculcate in your children, proper values and logical thinking, then minimalism will spring from there.

For example: don't just say "no" to a request for a nifty new gadget. Tell them your reasons for not allowing the purchase. Kids may seem like they are not listening but they are! You'll be surprised!

Minimalism and Your Budget

Let's get it out in the open. 9 out of 10 times, a minimalist lifestyle will result in daily or even weekly savings. However, as you progress in your endeavor, you will also be making some pretty hefty purchases i.e. solar panels, methane gas production, rain catchment facility, a bicycle, woodworking tools, etc. These purchases will allow you to be self sufficient and save more money in the long run though. But that's months, or even years from now. Today, you want to concentrate on cutting your grocery list, gas allowance, luxury items and premium services (i.e. cable, internet, telephone, etc.).

Tip: Create an expense worksheet. Version 1 need not be arranged. All you need to do is list down ALL things/services that cost you money. Now, with that list as a basis, separate the products and services into needs and wants. For example, you need electricity but you want cable. You need a cellular phone line, but you want to have the higher postpaid plan. Version 3 requires you to minimize your utility bills i.e. gas, electric, water, heat, etc.

Emotional Baggage

Every person carries with him/her emotional baggage i.e. unfulfilled wishes, displeased relatives, lost love, etc. The trick is differentiating between emotions that need more work and emotions that you need to let go. For example, forgiving your parent/s and starting things anew can lead to a more peaceful future. Letting go of a relationship that did not work, allows you to be more open to new love/s.

There is also the question of not overly obsessing on closure. If the other party does not want to communicate with you and work things out, then ample and sincere efforts are enough. Sometimes you need to give up on things to find closure.

The bottom line is; you should consider things within and without your control. Be realistic and leave a little bit of wiggle room. Work your way slowly into a perceived minimalism goal. Think of it as a marathon and not a 100 meter dash. The former puts emphasis on going the distance and finishing what you started. The latter is simply doing it as fast as you can, thinking, it will be over with quickly.

Chapter 4: Moving Past the Clutter

After you have looked internally, removed unnecessary thoughts, and emotional baggage, it is time to start re-arranging your surroundings to suite your belief and lifestyle. Below are a few ideas you should consider. Most are centered around your home, work station, bedroom, etc.

Work Station

How does your workstation or home office look like? To be quite honest, do not think that the end result will be a picture perfect work desk. That's just for commercials and print ad. If it's the case, then you probably aren't doing much work. In reality, a person who is into his work and is productive day in and day out will always have a certain degree of clutter lying around. The important thing is to sort things out properly and to de clutter on a day to day basis. Below are a few tips to remember.

- In and Out tray/bin. Dedicate specific areas of your workstation for in and out. This way you can tangibly see if there is and how much work there is left to be done.

- Tidy up before and after: Before you start your day, make a few adjustments. Before you leave your workstation clean your mess. The former simulates control and is a very good pre work ritual. The later is a signal to your brain that your day is done.

- Leave your worries in the office. This is easier said than done, especially if you are the owner/co-owner or in any capacity financially invested in the company. At the very least, make an active effort! Eventually you'll get the hang of it!

De Cluttering Your Home

This is a big task to perform in toto. The trick is to divide the work and celebrate smaller achievements. The author suggests, you work one room at a time. Best if finish one room in 1 or two continuous sessions. No one has to tell you that things that need work in the house have a tendency of piling up. It's a tossup between the living room and the bedroom. Personally the author prefers that you start with your bedroom because it is a more personal space.

Bedrooms

Divide your task into sections of the room and specific items. For example, it is a generally a good idea to start on the drawers, and with the clothes first. Box up clothes, accessories, shoes, etc. that have not been used for at least a year. Consult with the room owner. Allow the same to select 10 safe items. Another option is to have a "safe box". This allows the room owner to place in a small to medium sized box, anything he/she does not want included in your mission to de-clutter. This means regardless of what it is and how useless it maybe, it will not get the boot! This applies to any item located in any place in the house! But only to the extent that it can fit the box and/or is a safe item. In other words, it should be within reason.

Loose Paper

Every room is littered with loose paper. This can be in the form receipts, calling cards, notes, etc. You need to let the owner of the room sort everything out. Pay special attention to receipts which serve as store warranties, tax purposes, budgeting, etc.

What's Underneath?

Look underneath the mattress, bed, drawers, tables, chairs, etc. These are usually places where items get forgotten to gather dust. Remember, a real minimalist does not say "out of sight out of mind".

Clothes and Linen

How many sets of lined do you really need? 2 to 3 sets per bed is enough! Anything more and you are just taking up space. Do this simple exercise: smell your stack of linen. Chances are halfway thru you'll smell dust and mould! Time to give to charity.

Comfort Items

This can be anything from a teddy bear, a ratty old shirt, some toys, etc. for example: be careful not to give away that favorite ratty shirt of your housemate. Remember the safe box? Well, if your household member forgot to place it there, remind the same. If the answer is still no, then you have the go signal. Again, anything not worn in over a year, usually goes. Particularly those clothes that have already been stained by dust, moulds, mildew, etc.

Toiletries

If your bedroom has a bathroom then you should get rid of unnecessary toiletries. Throw out anything that smells funky and looks disgusting. Give the owner of the toiletry an ultimatum! Oh and look for the expiration date!

Books and Magazines

This is a tricky part. The general rule is, if the book is related to your business or is part of a professional library, then just arrange it properly. Ask the owner of the book on what can be let go. If you've got plenty of books and are confident of your DIY skills, then make a wall to wall shelf

You can be a bit more liberal with magazines. Be careful about job related magazines like medical and legal journals, design and fashion magazines, architecture related, etc.

Gadgets and Gizmos

Realistically speaking every household member has an old piece of electronic device he/she stores away. This can be anything form an old pc, mobile phone, CRT television, transistor radio, laser disc player, etc. With the possible exemption of the transistor radio which can be used for emergencies, most other electronics must go. Heck, you can even sell some online. Just makes sure to take out the memory cards or the hard drive, for anything that may contain sensitive information. Remember, sometimes erasing the data is not enough for professional and personal data!

The Kitchen

You'd be surprised, but the kitchen is a hotspot for clutter. Start with the big things then move down to the smaller utensils. For example, how many pots do you really need? Unless you are a prolific cook 6 pots are plenty i.e. 1 frying pan, small, medium, large stew pots, a wok, grill/skillet, etc. Give away old pots that are no longer being used. If you are still using old pots and pans when you have a fresh and expensive set on display, why not live for the moment and use the latter! You can always buy newer ones!

How many utensils do you really need? It's absurd having several dozen spoons and forks when you're household only comprise of six or less. Even counting potential guests you only need 2 dozen at most. Do you really need all those knives, strainers, graters, slicers, dicers, etc.? Chances are you should throw out old ones and use the ones you have in storage.

The Refrigerator

Defrost your refrigerator or at least shut it down (no frost) and perform a thorough cleaning. This means removing everything inside and wiping the refrigerator down with bleach laced water. Now throw out half consumed bottles, cans, zip lock bags that look and smell funky. Anything else that is consumable should be eaten by you and your family. You can also give it to a homeless person you see. Don't forget the top of the refrigerator.

Cupboard Cleaning

How much clutter is inside your cupboard? Throw away expired foodstuff and then use a smart storage system to tidy up your cupboard. Combine the same kind of food i.e. starch, flour, corn meal, cereal, sugar, coffee, salt, etc.

Dining Room

In most cases, you just want a spic and span dining area. Very minimal items displayed on the dining table; probably a couple of fruits, bread, and finger foods to nibble on. There are two rules here. One, your dining table should always be cleaned off anything that is not remotely related to food. Second, used spoons, forks, plates, glasses, etc. should be cleaned immediately and placed in the cupboard.

Living Room

Your living room needs to have 3 things. The first is a central piece wherein all your household members can huddle together. Second are a couple of family pictures. Third, is plenty of leg room. Keep that in mind when you are arranging the same. By doing so, you minimize the importance of the television set, dozens, if not hundreds of CD's, magazines, throw pillows, scented candles, etc.

Basement/Attic/Garage

Chances are this is where you store your clutter. You may do so in nifty containers. But clutter is clutter. You don't need to have those broken pieces of furniture. You don't need to keep your old CRT television set. You don't need to keep old bicycles or non functioning motor vehicles. Throw, give, sell those excess items.

Lawn/Garden, etc.

Keeping things simple does not mean boring and dull. A true minimalist utilizes everything around him/her. Keep the grass green and the surrounding trees properly trimmed. Regularly rake debris from your lawn. Clean out the clutter in your garden shed. A fresh coat of paint can do wonders for the same.

Halfway House

If you need more time to get rid of your clutter, you can rent a storage unit. Don't relax once you've shipped out your excess things. You need to actively sell and give to charity. The author suggests, that you decide on a deadline. Say, 6 months after storage and actively pursue it!

Cooking the Minimalist Way

Yup, cooking also involves minimalism. Avoid unnecessary ingredients as well as unnecessary use of pots, pans, utensils, etc. for example, why not use 1 pan to fry your bacon, stir fry veggies then make scrambled eggs? This way you cook faster and have less to clean up.

Chapter 5: Minimalist Life Hacks

To help you de clutter your home, the author has compiled several useful tips and techniques. Let's start:

General Clean Up

While rearranging your home, you might as well perform a general cleaning. Yup this means every nook and cranny! You should also be prepared with a couple of dozen organizing boxes, duct tape, plastic bags, etc. Don't forget to label everything before closing the sealing the lid.

Be Systematic

Clean and de-clutter in one continuous direction i.e. top to bottom then left to right, This provides you with a sense of continuity and minimizes the chances of dust getting transferred from one place to another. Don't forget to recycle when de-cluttering your home! This also means sorting out the things you give, sell and throw away.

Become a Builder

Learn to do it yourself. Let us face it, some store bought items are expensive and sometimes substandard. If you are good with your hands, you can build your own storage space at a fraction of the cost. You can grow your own fruits and veggies on your backyard. How does a hanging garden sound like? Some minimalists are even known to design and build their own furniture!

Commune with Nature

A minimalist should learn what it feels like to live with the barest essentials. This allows you to be thankful of what you have and realize that you really don't need much in order to live happy and be comfortable. One way of driving this point home is to go camping.

Don't camp with armatures. Camp with real honest to goodness experts like hikers, trekkers, mountaineers, trail guides, etc. Stress the importance of finding satisfaction with minimal material possessions.

You'll be surprised, how out in the wild, a simple porridge or stew can taste so good and be so filling! This is, as opposed to when you are eating the same or even a tastier variant in a luxurious home.

For the more advanced and/or adventurous, you might even like to take a page from the CEO of Facebook. He figured that, in order to appreciate what he eats, he has to pick the fruits, veggies and hunt the meat that goes into some of the meals he eats. Say, once a month.

Conclusion

Thank you again for downloading this book!

I hope this book was able to help you to understand true minimalism and bring you closer to a more natural way of life. A life with less clutter, involves less consumption and maximum personal growth.

The next step is to keep at it. Think of your life as a minimalist as an upward spiral, NOT a circle. Why a spiral. This is because, a spiral signifies a continuous cycle that, when done right results in you moving slowly up and finding ways to better yourself. On the other hand, a circle merely refers to a repetitive cycle in which you never progress.

Finally, if you enjoyed this book, please take the time to share your thoughts and post a review on Amazon. It'd be greatly appreciated!

Thank you and good luck!

www.ingramcontent.com/pod-product-compliance
Lightning Source LLC
Chambersburg PA
CBHW070258290526
45789CB00004B/1890